THE WANTS OF MAN · A POEM

John Quincy Adams.

THE WANTS OF MAN

A POEM

BY JOHN QUINCY ADAMS

Written in 1840, first published in 1841, frequently reprinted, and now reissued with an Introduction by L. H. Butterfield, and published by

IMPRINT SOCIETY · 1972

BARRE · MASSACHUSETTS

NOTE ON THE FRONTISPIECE

The worried countenance in the frontispiece is that of our poet not long after he had composed "The Wants of Man" but looking as if many of his own wants were far from satisfied. This is the John Quincy Adams of the bruising fights in Congress during the 1840's, deeply concerned for the fate of his country and of his kind. The likeness is reproduced from an engraving (in the Edes Collection, Massachusetts Historical Society) by William Wellstood (1819–1900), copyright by the New York firm of Johnson, Fry & Co. in 1857, but Wellstood worked from a daguerreotype (of which only photographic and engraved versions appear to exist) that has been authoritatively attributed to Mathew Brady. See Andrew Oliver, *Portraits of John Quincy Adams and His Wife* (Cambridge, 1970), Chapter 6.

© 1972 IMPRINT SOCIETY
All rights reserved
Library of Congress Catalog Card Number 70–185754
International Standard Book Number 0–87636–032–0
Printed in the United States of America

INTRODUCTION

It was once well known, though it has long since been forgotten — and perhaps excusably — that John Quincy Adams aspired to fame as a poet. Among his papers in the Massachusetts Historical Society is a vast literary miscellany that includes verse composition books beginning in 1784, when he was sixteen or seventeen, and extending until his death in 1848, when he was approaching eighty-one. Some of these run to hundreds of closely written pages. Among them are several versions of his translation of Wieland's *Oberon*, which date from his diplomatic mission to Berlin in the later 1790's and were the means by which he mastered the German language. There is a very long original narrative poem in Byronic stanzas (though it points a very non-Byronic moral), entitled *Dermot MacMorrogh*, on a theme in Irish medieval history. When the publisher called for the author's corrections for another printing of his "epic," Adams was surprised and pleased; he knew, he said, that it was not a very good epic, but what other American statesman had written an epic at all? Still later, Adams whiled away the hours of tedious debates in the House of Representatives by versifying the Psalms, and at times the leaves of his manuscript diary in the 1830's are mostly devoted to heavily corrected eight-line stanzas, with his record of the proceedings in the House cramped into one third or so of each page.

Above all, in these later years, Adams indulged in the diversion of writing album verse. It was an age of sentiment; it was an age of autograph collecting. Embattled as he was in Congress over such issues as slavery and the slave trade, the right of popular petition, and the establishment of the Smithsonian Institution on a truly scientific footing rather than as a rest home for broken-down politicians, Adams found relief in composing verses. They were always on moral themes, but they usually had an epigrammatic polish; and sometimes a gleam of humor still shines through their stilted language and tinkling meter. Finding them admired, he was flattered into producing more, virtually on demand, for the wives and daughters of members of Congress — even of members with whom, during sessions of the House, he might be locked in deadly combat.

Though he worked as hard on them as he did on his speeches designed to save the union of American states, Adams did not overrate his poetical productions. "I have kept copies of all my contributions to albums," he remarked in his diary in 1839, "and I sicken at the sight of them." But he went on writing them, and it was in order to meet a kind of mass demand that, as he recorded on

8 May 1840, "I rode home [from the Capitol], and wasted a great part of the evening ... writing verses on the wants of man." Again, next day: "I finished last night almost sleepless, and this morning my verses upon the wants of man. I suppose it is my intense anxiety for the Bill now under my charge which bereaves me of sleep, and the composition of verses, trifling upon another [subject], is the only mode of relieving myself from the continual pressure upon the brain of thought upon one subject, through a sleepless night."

Actually his poem was by no means done. As the debates on his revenue bill grew more intense, Adams' insomnia grew worse and he added more stanzas. After all, the wants of man are unlimited. Composition was also protracted, though not stopped, by Adams' tripping, a few days later, on some newly laid matting in the House and dislocating his right shoulder. In a halting hand he described this incident fully in his diary entry of the next day and interpreted it as an admonition of "Providence" to get on with his duties. "The Wants of Man," in twenty-five stanzas, was finished in mid-June, although the author had already given away single stanzas and shorter versions of it in his own hand to autograph hunters who couldn't wait for its completion.

A copy he gave in June 1840 to Congressman Christopher Morgan of Auburn, New York, came to the notice, some time later, of Mrs. William H. Seward, wife of the governor of New York State. She was so pleased with it that she sought permission to have it published. Adams complied, and a copy was furnished to Thurlow Weed's Albany *Evening Journal,* where "The Wants of Man" appeared in print for the first time on 3 September 1841, with a headnote similar to that at the head of the present text. On 8 September the Washington *National Intelligencer* reprinted the poem, with an additional stanza (No. VIII in the present text) which Adams had written very recently and must have furnished separately to the editor. Any number of other papers soon did likewise. An enterprising printer in Lowell, Massachusetts, issued a chapbook or paperback edition which is now rare but has been found with both 1841 and 1842 imprint dates. "The Wants of Man" is placed first in the (unauthorized) collection of Adams' *Poems of Religion and Society* which was published in the year of his death and went through several editions. Editors of magazines and gift books of course picked it up, and compilers of anthologies reprinted it, wholly or in part, at intervals throughout the rest of the century. Thus this poetical effusion, "chance-begotten," as its author said, "to make autographs for poor Charles Ogle's note-paper," may have been printed more often than any other separate composition John Quincy Adams ever wrote. The most recent edition was issued ten years ago in miniature form printed by Joh. Enschedé en Zonen in Haarlem over the imprint of

Achille J. St. Onge of Worcester, Massachusetts, with an introduction, here reprinted with corrections, by the present writer. It is now out of print.

"Trifling" as Adams more than once called it, "The Wants of Man" tells a certain amount about both its author and the age in which it was written. Adams' true monument as a writer is his diary, which he kept for nearly seventy years and which is without a serious rival in its field. But that was a private record, and, like most mortals, even John Quincy Adams hungered for public approval. "I want the voice of honest praise," he said in this poem, and meant it; but compared with other political leaders of his stature he got very little. So he worked his small talent for versification hard and was inwardly delighted when what he wrote caught the fancy of friends and, eventually, of the reading public. Modern readers will find the jingling rhythm, the appalling inversions of word order, the periphrases that even by 1840 were old-fashioned, the elephantine humor, and the heavy piety of the poem a little staggering, and will wonder why it was ever admired. It was admired, of course, because it was in the gift-book, album-sentiment taste of the day; and the inventory of house furnishings and *objets d'art* "wanted" is a manual of interior decoration on the most opulent scale in the early Victorian era. But more to the point, several stanzas toward the close of the poem are charged with a moral earnestness that typifies John

Quincy Adams the statesman and the man. If one knows anything of Adams' long and ultimately successful struggle against Southern gags on the right of petition for the abolition of slavery, one cannot laugh off his prayer for

> A tongue to speak at Virtue's need
> In Heaven's sublimest strain;
> And lips, the cause of Man to plead,
> And never plead in vain.

The text of the edition in hand is based on the first separate publication, *The Wants of Man; A Poem, by John Quincy Adams*, Lowell: Amos Lupton, 1841, a chapbook of fifteen pages in buff paper covers, in size only 4⅜ by 3 1/10 inches. As printers do, Lupton normalized Adams' spelling, capitalization, and punctuation, and he not only copied previous printers' mistakes but made some more himself. The present text has therefore been corrected by a comparison with the only holograph version currently known, one presented on 23 August 1841 to Congressman William C. Dawson of Georgia (and now in the deCoppet Collection in the Princeton University Library); with the first printing in the Albany *Evening Journal*, 3 September 1841; and with two later newspaper printings that had the benefit of Adams' oversight — in the *Daily National Intelligencer*, of Washington, 8 September, and in the Quincy, Massachusetts, *Patriot*, 25 September 1841. The result is an eclectic text, but it embodies all of Adams' additions and final revisions.

Since he produced so many, there must be other whole and partial texts of "The Wants of Man" extant in the author's hand. The editors of *The Adams Papers*, now in course of publication by The Belknap Press of Harvard University Press, would be glad to learn about them, or indeed about any manuscript writings and letters by or to members of the Adams family that may have escaped their notice. Information of this kind is essential to the success of the editorial work and will be warmly welcomed if sent to the editors at the Massachusetts Historical Society, 1154 Boylston Street, Boston, Massachusetts.

L. H. BUTTERFIELD

THE WANTS OF MAN

> Man wants but little here below,
> Nor wants that little long.
> GOLDSMITH'S *Hermit*

THE FOLLOWING poem was written in July, 1840 [actually in May and June 1840, with later revisions and additions], under these circumstances: Gen. Ogle [Charles Ogle, member of Congress from Somerset, Pennsylvania] informed Mr. Adams that several young ladies in his district had requested him to obtain Mr. A's *autograph* for them. In accordance with this request, Mr. Adams wrote the following beautiful poem upon "The Wants of Man," each stanza upon a sheet of note paper. What American young lady would not set a precious value upon such an autograph from this illustrious statesman?

Introductory note in the first separate printing, Lowell, 1841

I

"Man wants but little here below,
 Nor wants that little long."
'Tis not with *me* exactly so —
 But 'tis so in the song.
My wants are many, and, if told,
 Would muster many a score;
And were each wish a mint of gold,
 I still should long for more.

II

What first I want is daily bread,
 And canvas-backs and wine;
And all the realms of Nature spread
 Before me when I dine.
Four courses scarcely can provide
 My appetite to quell,
With four choice cooks from France beside,
 To dress my dinner well.

III

What next I want, at heavy cost,
    Is elegant attire;
Black sable furs for winter's frost,
    And silks for summer's fire,
And Cashmere shawls, and Brussels lace,
    My bosom's front to deck,
And diamond rings my hands to grace,
    And rubies for my neck.

IV

And then I want a mansion fair,
    A dwelling house, in style;
Four stories high, for wholesome air—
    A massive marble pile;
With halls for banquets and for balls,
    All furnish'd rich and fine;
With stabled steeds in fifty stalls,
    And cellars for my wine.

V

I want a garden and a park
    My dwelling to surround,
A thousand acres (bless the mark!),
    With walls encompass'd round,
Where flocks may range and herds may low,
    And kids and lambkins play;
And flowers and fruits commingled grow,
    All Eden to display.

VI

I want, when summer's foliage falls,
    And autumn strips the trees,
A house within the city's walls
    For comfort and for ease —
But here, as space is somewhat scant,
    And acres somewhat rare,
My house in town I only want
    To occupy — a Square.

VII

I want a steward, butler, cooks,
    A coachman, footmen, grooms;
A library of well-bound books,
    And picture-garnish'd rooms;
Correggio's Magdalen and Night,
    The Matron of the chair;
Guido's fleet coursers in their flight,
    And Claudes, at least a pair.

VIII

Ay, and to stamp my form and face
    Upon the solid rock,
I want, their lineaments to trace,
    Carrara's milk-white block.
And let the chisel's art sublime,
    By Greenough's hand display,
Through all the range of future time,
    My features to the day.

IX

I want a cabinet profuse
    Of medals, coins, and gems;
A printing press for private use
    Of fifty thousand *ems;*
And plants, and minerals, and shells;
    Worms, insects, fishes, birds;
And every beast on earth that dwells
    In solitude or herds.

X

I want a board of burnish'd plate,
    Of silver and of gold;
Tureens of twenty pounds in weight,
    With sculpture's richest mould;
Plateaus, with chandeliers and lamps,
    Plates, dishes, all the same;
And porcelain vases with the stamps
    Of Sevres and Angouleme.

XI

And maples curl'd of glossy stain
    Must form my chamber doors,
And carpets of the Wilton grain
    Must cover all my floors;
My walls, with tapestry bedeck'd,
    Must never be outdone;
And damask curtains must protect
    Their colors from the sun.

XII

And mirrors of the largest pane
    From Venice must be brought;
And sandal-wood and bamboo-cane
    For chairs and tables bought.
On all the mantel-pieces, clocks
    Of thrice-gilt bronze must stand,
And screens of ebony and box
    Invite the stranger's hand.

XIII

I want (who does not want?) a wife,
    Affectionate and fair,
To solace all the woes of life,
    And all its joys to share;
Of temper sweet—of yielding will—
    Of firm, yet placid mind;
With all my faults to love me still,
    With sentiment refin'd.

XIV

And as Time's car incessant runs,
    And Fortune fills my store,
I want of daughters and of sons
    From eight to half a score.
I want (alas! can mortal dare
    Such bliss on earth to crave?)
That all the girls be chaste and fair—
    The boys all wise and brave.

XV

And when my bosom's darling sings
    With melody divine,
A pedal harp of many strings
    Must with her voice combine.
A piano, exquisitely wrought,
    Must open stand, apart,
That all my daughters may be taught
    To win the stranger's heart.

XVI

My wife and daughters will desire
    Refreshment from perfumes,
Cosmetics for the skin require,
    And artificial blooms.
The civet, fragrance shall dispense,
    And treasur'd sweets return;
Cologne revive the flagging sense,
    And smoking amber burn.

XVII

And when, at night, my weary head
    Begins to droop and dose,
A southern chamber holds my bed
    For Nature's soft repose;
With blanket, counterpane, and sheet,
    Mattrass, and bed of down,
And comfortables for my feet,
    And pillows for my crown.

XVIII

I want a warm and faithful friend
    To cheer the adverse hour,
Who ne'er to flatter will descend,
    Nor bend the knee to power;
A friend to chide me when I'm wrong,
    My inmost soul to see;
And that my friendship prove as strong
    For him, as his for me.

XIX

I want a kind and tender heart,
    For others' wants to feel;
A soul secure from Fortune's dart,
    And bosom arm'd with steel,
To bear divine chastisement's rod;
    And mingling in my plan,
Submission to the will of God
    With charity to Man.

XX

I want a keen, observing eye,
    An ever-listening ear,
The truth through all disguise to spy,
    And wisdom's voice to hear;
A tongue to speak at Virtue's need
    In Heaven's sublimest strain;
And lips, the cause of Man to plead,
    And never plead in vain.

XXI

I want uninterrupted health
    Throughout my long career,
And never-failing streams of wealth
    To scatter far and near;
The destitute to clothe and feed,
    Free bounty to bestow;
Supply the helpless orphan's need,
    And soothe the widow's woe.

XXII

I want the genius to conceive,
    The talents to unfold
Designs, the vicious to retrieve,
    The virtuous to uphold;
Inventive power, combining skill,
    Persuasion's soft control,
Of human hearts to mould the will,
    And reach from Pole to Pole.

XXIII

I want the seals of power and place,
>   The ensigns of command,
Charg'd by the People's unbought grace,
>   To rule my native land —
Nor crown, nor sceptre would I ask,
>   But from my Country's will,
By day, by night, to ply the task
>   Her cup of bliss to fill.

XXIV

I want the voice of honest praise
>   To follow me behind;
And to be thought in future days
>   The friend of human kind,
That after ages, as they rise,
>   Exulting may proclaim
In choral union to the skies
>   Their blessings on my name.

XXV

These are the wants of mortal man;
    I cannot want them long—
For life itself is but a span,
    And earthly bliss a song.
My last great *want*, absorbing all,
    Is, when beneath the sod,
And summon'd to my final call,
    The *mercy of my God*.

XXVI

And oh! while circles in my veins
    Of life the purple stream,
And yet a fragment small remains
    Of Nature's transient dream,
My soul, in humble hope, unscar'd,
    Forget not thou to pray,
That this thy *want* may be prepar'd
    To meet the Judgment Day.

C O L O P H O N

A limited edition of one-thousand copies of this presentation book have been printed at the press of A. Colish. The typefaces are Baskerville for the text with Bulmer for display. The paper is white laid Curtis Rag. The frontispiece was reproduced by The Meriden Gravure Company from an engraving of a daguerreotype attributed to Mathew Brady. The binding is by the Sendor Bindery. Joseph Blumenthal designed the book.

This is copy number